At the Lake

Robbie Byerly

At the lake, we saw the water.

At the lake, we saw the trees.

3

 At the lake, we saw the rocks.

At the lake, we saw the turtle.

 At the lake, we saw the frog.

At the lake, we saw the fish.

8

At the lake, we saw the duck.

At the lake, we saw the eggs.

9

 **At the lake, we saw the boats.**

At the lake, we saw the bench.

At the lake, we saw the bikes.

At the lake, we saw the man.

14

At the lake, we saw the kites.

At the lake, we saw the dog. 15

I can match the word to the picture using the first letter sound.

trees

dog

rocks

fish

16